MW00681619

To:
From:

Written and compiled by Todd Hafer.

ISBN 978-1-61626-637-0

Cover and interior design: Kirk DouPonce, DogEared Design
Cover and interior illustrations: Jody Williams

Published by Barbour Publishing, Inc., P.O. Box 719, Uhrichsville, Ohio 44683, www.barbourbooks.com

Our mission is to publish and distribute inspirational products offering exceptional value and biblical encouragement to the masses.

Printed in India.

I want you to know. . .

GRAD,

you're

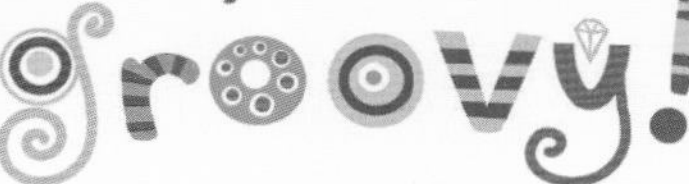

BARBOUR
PUBLISHING

We count as blessed
those who have persevered.

JAMES 5:11 NIV

Grad, you're

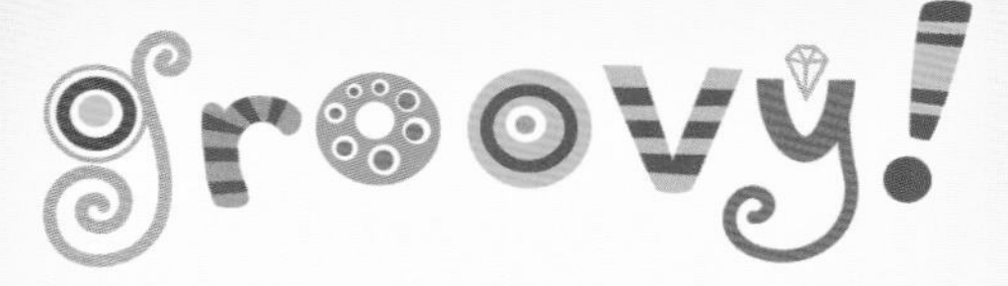

because...

life has a lot to offer you—
and you have a lot to offer life!

Grad, you're
groovy!
because...

you've learned a
ton of cool stuff!

Grad, you're

because...

you've learned how to *learn*!

Grad, you're
groovy!
because...

you kept believing in yourself,
even when things got tough.

Grad, you're

because...

after every ending comes
a bright new beginning!

Grad, you're
groovy!
because...

you know that sometimes
the greatest ability is availability!

You must begin wherever you are.

JACK BOLAND

Grad, you're

because...

you've tackled one of
life's toughest challenges!

Grad, you're
groovy!
because...

no matter what you end up
becoming, you'll always be YOU!
(And you are awesome!)

Grad, you're

because...

you kept going when
others might have quit.

Grad, you're
groovy!
because...

even when life took
you on a detour,
you found a way to
enjoy the scenery.

Grad, you're

because...

even though people look
alike in those caps and gowns,
you have a way of standing
out from the crowd!

Grad, you're
groovy!
because...

you've set a good example
for the younger people
who look up to you.

It is not a successful climb
unless you enjoy the journey.

Dan Benson

Grad, you're

because...

you know that work and
play can be best friends!

Grad, you're
groovy!
because...

you understand
that every calling
is great when
it's greatly pursued!

Grad, you're

because...

you've proven that (sometimes)
sleep is overrated!

Grad, you're

because...

you've vanquished the foes
known as Fear, Doubt, and Fatigue.

Grad, you're
groovy!
because...

you've made so many
people so very proud of you!

Grad, you're

because...

you know that to succeed,
sometimes you gotta improvise!

It's kind of fun
to do the impossible.

WALT DISNEY

Grad, you're
groovy!
because...

you can do the common stuff
in an uncommon way!

Grad, you're

because...

you left your school a
better place than it was
when you entered.

Grad, you're
groovy!
because...

you bring something
beautiful to the world—
something no one else can offer.

Grad, you're

because...

you know that every day is
a wonderful chance to become
what you've dreamed.

Grad, you're
groovy!
because...

you embrace your dreams
with both passion and purpose!

Grad, you're

groovy!

because...

you don't wait
for opportunities—
you create 'em!

Nothing splendid has ever been achieved except by those who dared believe that something inside them was superior to circumstance.

Bruce Barton

Grad, you're

because...

you face fears rather than
hide from them.

Grad, you're

groovy!

because...

you're living proof that
God answers prayer!

Grad, you're

because...

you know the first
step to success is
believing you can succeed.

Grad, you're
groovy!
because...

your smiles of accomplishment
make me smile, too!

Grad, you're

because...

you've shown that one
of the best tools for
success is a sense of humor!

Grad, you're

because...

you've shown that a person
can do almost anything
with prayer, hard work,
and the right amount of coffee!

Endeavor to live so
that when you die, even the
undertaker will be sorry.

MARK TWAIN

Grad, you're
groovy!
because...

you know that small
opportunities are often the
beginning of great enterprises.

Grad, you're

because...

you've learned that the
tassel is worth the hassle!

Grad, you're

because...

you've made more than grades—
you've made friends!

Grad, you're

because...

when opportunity knocks,
you don't pretend you're not home!

Grad, you're
groovy!
because...

you've gotten what everyone
wants out of school—outta there!

Grad, you're

because...

you're not afraid
to ask questions.

Get out there and give real help!
Get out there and love!
Get out there and testify!
Get out there and create whatever
you can to inspire people.

Mother Teresa

Grad, you're
groovy!
because...

you not only set goals—
you achieve them!

Grad, you're

because...

you know that the
dreams of the future trump
the history of the past.

Grad, you're
groovy!
because...

you've done your part
to support the
highlighter industry!

Grad, you're

because...

even when you're not at school,
you still have class!

Grad, you're
groovy!
because...

you've stayed awake through
lectures that would have put
a mere mortal in a coma!

Grad, you're

because...

you know that two of the
most beautiful words in the English
language are "Class dismissed."

Success is often
just an idea away.

Frank Tyger

Grad, you're
groovy!
because...

you've done your part
to support the microwavable
popcorn industry!

Grad, you're

because...

you've made an art form
of eating on the run.

Grad, you're
groovy!
because...

you know the definition
of a true optimist:
the student who always
thinks class will get out early.

Grad, you're

because...

you know that, in a pinch,
a chocolate chip cookie,
a slice of cold pizza,
or a half a can of energy
drink can be breakfast!

Grad, you're

because...

you've faced changing times
with unchanging principles.

Grad, you're
groovy!
because...

you got your grades
the old-fashioned way:
you earned them!

Most folks are about
as happy as they make up
their minds to be.

ABRAHAM LINCOLN

Grad, you're

because...

you don't let what you
cannot do interfere with
what you CAN do!

Grad, you're
groovy!
because...

you understand that,
technically, ordering pizza
counts as "cooking."

Grad, you're

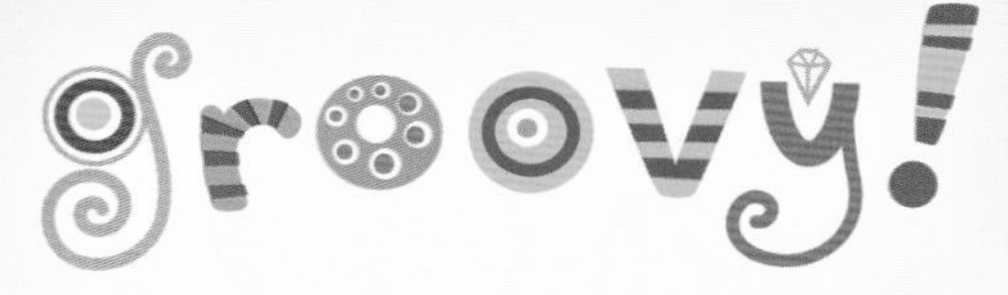

because...

you know that each
of life's setbacks is an
opportunity to discover what
you're really made of!

Grad, you're
groovy!
because...

you cherish your yesterdays,
dream your tomorrows,
and live your todays!

Grad, you're

groovy!

because...

you went to school
to learn, not to loaf!

Grad, you're

because...

you measure your success
by the amount of happiness
in your heart.

Grad, you're
groovy!
because...

you know the world
always looks brighter
from behind a smile!

To travel hopefully is a better thing than to arrive.

Robert Louis Stevenson

Grad, you're

because...

you know that one key
to success is to move from failure
to failure without losing hope.

Grad, you're

because...

you know that a “study break”
should never be longer
than the actual studying!

Grad, you're
groovy!
because...

you drank deeply from the
Fountain of Knowledge—
when some others
were only gargling!

Grad, you're

because...

you know that if at first you
DO succeed, you should
try not to look too surprised!

Grad, you're
groovy!
because...

you're not afraid
of terrifying things—
like pop quizzes
and mystery meat!

Grad, you're

because...

you've come to understand
that if you love learning,
learning tends to
love you back!

Personality can open doors,
but only character can keep them open.

Elmer G. Leterman

Grad, you're

because...

you know that if you
don't control your schedule,
your schedule will control you!

Grad, you're
groovy!
because...

you're learning that gratitude
is the key to happiness.

Grad, you're

because...

you know that school is like
being a military leader—you have to
pick your battles carefully!

Grad, you're

because...

you know that every failure
is simply an opportunity
to begin again, more intelligently.

Grad, you're

because...

you know that doing what
you love enriches the soul.

Grad, you're
groovy!
because...

you have learned that life's
rainbows follow life's storms.

There are only two
ways to live your life.
One is as though
nothing is a miracle.
The other is as though
everything is a miracle.

ALBERT EINSTEIN